EAR

&

OTHER

POEMS

By

PETER KENNEDY

Copyright © PETER KENNEDY 2023
This book is sold subject to the condition that it shall not, by
way of trade or otherwise, be lent, resold, hired out, or otherwise
circulated without the publisher's prior consent in any form of
binding or cover other than that in which it is published and
without a similar condition including this condition being
imposed on the subsequent publisher.
The moral right of PETER KENNEDY has been asserted.
ISBN-13: 9798864934654

For my friends Frances and Laurence Boxer

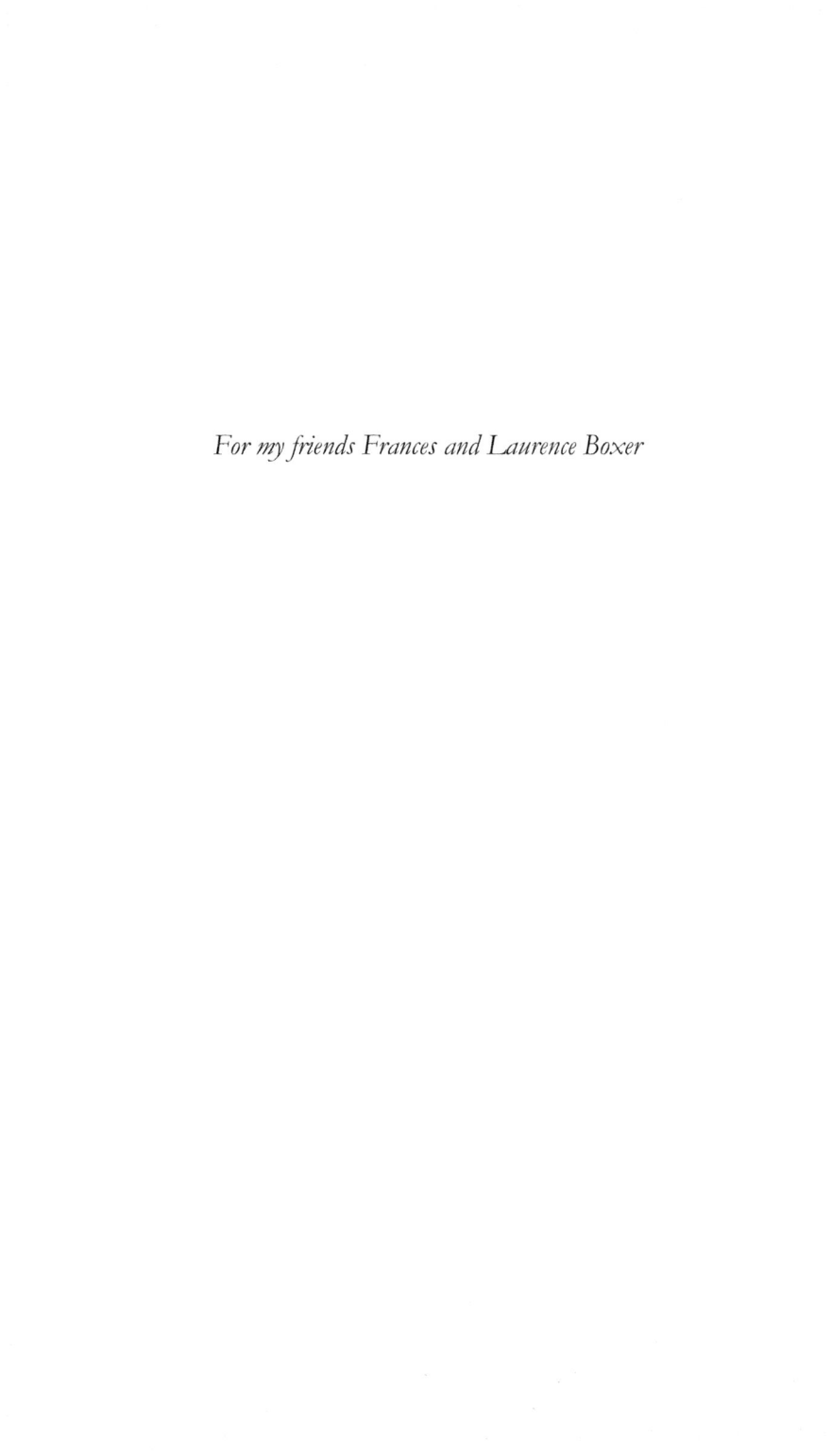

CONTENTS

ABSOLUTE FEAR 1
ALTRUISM RULES 3
AN IMAGINED LOSS 5
CANCER 6
COAST IN SUMMER.. 7
COMPASSION 8
CONCERT PERFORMANCE 9
DEPENDENCE.. 10
DREAMING... 11
EARTH TIME.. 12
EVASIVE TRUTH 14
FATAL ILLNESS 15
FOREIGN EXPERIENCE.. 16
HALCYON TIMES.. 17
HARD ADVICE 18
IN MEMORIAM.. 19
LAKE AND MOUNTAINS 20
LEGACY AND LIVING 21
MAGIC MOUNTAIN 22
MALIGNANT FUTURE 23
MEDICAL EMERGENCE 24
MEDICAL WISDOM 25
MOON FEVER 26
NIGHT WATCH 27
NOSTALGIC RIVER... 28
OCEAN VIEW 29
OUT OF THE WORLD 31
PONDERING CREATION 32
RETROSPECTIVE JUDGEMENT 33

ROUGH TRAINING	34
RUSTIC FERVOUR	35
SEA BREAKER	37
SOULFUL VIRTUOSITY	38
SPORTS	39
SUNSHINE RULES	40
THE MAGPIE	41
THE OBSERVERS	42
THE PATIENT AND HIS FEAR	43
THE PHYSICIAN	44
THE PLAYERS	45
THE SEAFRONT	46
THE THROW	47
THEN AND NOW	48
THINKING	49
ABOUT THE AUTHOR	50

ABSOLUTE FEAR

Waiting for fear to descend in this room
And shroud my life in cruel uncertainty
All the faith that resides in this poor soul
Finds itself emerging in cold terror.
A prick, a scratch, a sleep without dreams
Must lead to a promised land of freedom
From a physical form of frailty
Forcing us back to grim reality

Living in times as these appears so sweet
This removal from normal existence
Only serves to reinforce life in full
Then brings us back to what now matters most.
The breaking up of a family chain
Whether parents, siblings, spouse or children
Also has the power to shock and shame
For what in their short lives we never claimed.

Who has not had the elemental fear
Of sitting on the runway soon to fly
All faith residing in just two people
Trained to the hilt but seldom close enough
To understand our clinging on to life
This fleeting evidence of survival.
At times like these we perceive our maker
Aware of our basic fragility

Forcing us to confront our final end
Other life failures have this same effect
Whatever the intrinsic rejection
By people, papers, life or something else
All tragedies have different outcomes.
At some dark stage in our limited lives
The harsh reality of life and death
Will hit all hard or haunt us in advance

ALTRUISM RULES

I once thought back to a lively past
Always enveloped by compassion.
Early visions of a pensioner
Not the youngest member of that tribe
But a helpless woman then ancient
Who couldn't pay her simple bus fare
Through sheer poverty or something else
I am still unable to fathom
Who explained her situation well
While all the time I so felt for her
And duly settled her difficulty.
Her sad voice and face gently thanked me

Why such people have this strange affect
I can only blame the human trait
Of kind empathy for fellow souls.
But these sad feelings are physical
So deep can the time wounds penetrate.
Our medical mentors taught us well
That our patients' maladies present
With body complaints but mental pain
So deep are the cancers now within
Or odd non-malignant diseases.
The damage has already been done
By the time our sympathy kicks in.

Are these human and benign views real?
Do they truly reflect all we feel?
Or is this just a taught reaction
Just a learned official lip service?
Maybe the truth is a hybrid call
A mixture of mind and emotion.
Whatever the underlying cause
Of this kind and unique trait of ours
This strange altruistic paradox
With little genetic advantage,
The plight of others, humans or not
Has the strength for us lose the plot

AN IMAGINED LOSS

A loss as great as it can possibly be
A son, a daughter, what emerges from you
Will now return to haunt us all in our dreams
Though that will almost certainly kill our days
Of hunkering down amidst the wind and fires.
Only in our minds do such horrors play fast
And loose within our finely battered souls.
We imagine, soon act, reach, and then aspire.

Of the many trials that humans may face
None comes near the imagined trauma of loss
That might one day predate their parent's demise
That might yet blight the remainder of their time.
But life contains mercy as well as horror
It can always surprise us despite our fear.
So live on and try hard to match our dread.
Everything around us speaks of happiness

CANCER

A sudden pain or subtle defect
Can play havoc with a sense of self
The usual mechanism of automatic life
Is dismembered and left to fester.
Sad optimism can no longer exist
Though a glimmer of hope emerges
To maintain a narrow grip on life.
How we humans like a good deception

But through the pain and vivid dreams
There is always a ray of unreality
A coping tool rather than a strategy.
A noble bearing and forlorn dignity
Do little to assuage the malignancy
The slow but sure total destruction
Of what was once a personality
But now reduced to just a memory

COAST IN SUMMER

Sky and cloud appear to merge between
The gentle crevices of evening mist.
The natural binding of sea and land
Beckons to us all and calmly sits
In judgement while summer fades.
Always enticing us to look and feel
Emotions that somehow seem to grow
As quickly as the seasons change.

Slowly now the vistas try to move
From mental image to distant vision
From static minds to moving skies
All eyes pointing to just one end
Which gently satisfies our desire
To match what we try to perceive
As realistic with a mindful eye.
All fantasies so easily become real.

COMPASSION

Of human qualities I most admire
It's compassion that always comes out first
This special aspect that may be unique
Is the goal to which most of us aspire.
First the fragile soul tripping on the bus
Who has just lost the fare on pain of death
An end which beckons, taunts, and then expires.
See the bullied school child wailing pity
Who seeks in vain to be treated gently.
And the colleague near to sad misery
Who only just manages to survive
Despite the absence of support from friends.
The city's down and out begs for our change
Though a moment's caring would answer well.
There is one common thread behind all this
The lack of empathy and compassion
Is plain for all we humans to witness

CONCERT PERFORMANCE

The elegiac sounds point to a world
Where living and beauty sit side by side
Where languid elegance meets loud music
And binds us all into a state of grace.
This world of feeling and admiration
For those magicians who serenade us
Embracing their forms of reality
Subtly converts the listeners to dreams.
Dreams of performing and those that appear
Now in some way immersed within our brains.
Some are real and others are fantasy
Yet all musical perceptions are right.
Now the soloist then the orchestra
Now we see and then we dream of beauty

DEPENDENCE

We are told to act bravely every time
In case life takes a downward turn.
In case we find ourselves bereft of all
That keeps us firmly on the rails
That allows some aspect of our lives
A modicum of personal integrity

Happiness can sometimes be enjoyed
Only in retrospect when all is done
When a lifetime partner is dead and gone
When life is composed of emptiness
And despair creeps slowly to the fore
When all is lost and everything missed.

But what can never be lost or forgotten
Are the sweet memories of past time
The intimate legacy of happiness
The cinema of all that is remembered
The strange but reliable healing act
That makes us hold onto kind reality.

A bridge, a green vista in the sunlight
Gently bathing past and future desires
That fired our lives in timeless ways
That somehow framed a golden hope.
That every moment should stay the same
Despite the certainty of time's passing.

DREAMING

Who has ever once slept without a dream
That strange hinterland between the senses?
The summary of a lifetime's trauma
Is subtly altered to please troubled souls.
Dreaming is still a mystery to all
Those who try hard to see and understand
Know nothing more about this enigma
Compared with those of us who try to know.
A wish fulfilment we are duly told
Explains this state of unreality
But nightmares can never answer in full
And only masochists would choose that path.
So long as humans continue this life
They will dream on and put living on hold

EARTH TIME

Every twig and tree however small
Will surely outlive our little lives
The ones we hold so dear and precious
Yet will always end beneath the earth.
Such thoughts as these are as perennial
As the Douglas firs and plants around
Our artificial wall of elegance
Of safety within the forest glades.

Whether bathed in wide autumnal colour
Or baking beneath the heat of summer
One just marvels at the size and strength
Of giant firs and oaks like guardians
Of the flowing river that runs below
And adds a noble backdrop to our view.
The sun that quickly flickers through the trees
Completes the illusion of endless time.

But a sense of the real slowly appears
To bring our bodies gently down to earth
The iconic vision within our minds
Is duly crushed and fragmented by time
Whose wounds go deep within our perception
Our sad tendency for self-deception.
We can never be blamed for admiring
Products of nature with such perfection.

But for this illusory fragment now
That so penetrates our every fibre
A sense of kindness pervades our souls
And permits us to suspend all belief.
Enjoyment is allowed for just a view
As we drink the fruits of earthlight's prime.
The subtle blending of sun and soil
Serve to enhance this distant sense of time.

How should we recall this haunting vision
This dazzling snapshot of natural tones?
The historic power of house and stone
In what was once the nation's capital
Somehow merges in a strange fusion
With the Birnam Oak and River Tay,
This sense of majesty that pervades
The earth, the forests and what is home

EVASIVE TRUTH

The thing in itself remains worthwhile
Kant's concept of knowledge still holds sway
But truth and reality are gone
Now we must see it only their way.
News has seldom had less importance
Or authority since no-one knows
What truly exists in this mad world
Where truth is lost and anything goes.

If you dare to question what is said
By those towing the official line
Then beware of what they will then do
To you and everything you hold dear
Your life, your death, your very essence
Will suffer greatly we should be clear.
No-one knows when this madness will end
But until it does keep your thoughts near.

FATAL ILLNESS

All of the wealth the world now contains
Has no remedy to cure this soul
Which has no hope

The malignancy that will kill him
Does not respect hard money or life
It knows no compassion

No amount of prayer or medicine
Will ever have a hope in this hell
Of sickness and despair

A month or two may yet be promised
To settle debts, love and the future
Just to tie them up

Even a bargain with the devil
Will not answer to this final fate
Waiting at the door

But slowly the truth of death arrives
To put an end to this misery
So everyone loses.

FOREIGN EXPERIENCE

All time seems to be suspended
In this strange Indochina land
Where the sweeping flags of colour
Ride alongside our tour of klongs,
The swift movement of riversides
Acting as backdrops to our minds.

Now we see the hungry catfish
Waiting patiently for our bread
Then suddenly to pounce once more
As they feed on what we discard.
The lees of what we imagined
Are rendered as next to nothing.

Gentle splashes soon wet our cheeks
To remind us of the dangers
The hidden depths of sudden death
That wait for the unsuspecting.
While flowing water gives us life
It promises much more besides.

Riverbank beauty now pervades
This new Bangkok experience
This subtle snapshot in our minds
That enthrals the collective throngs.
Crimson flagpoles remain and fix
Visions we try so hard to find.

HALCYON TIMES

There was once a time for living and joy
Benevolent freedom was felt by all.
Childhood idylls are just a memory
And never known by today's progeny.
Though distant recall can sometimes lie
And some of those halcyon winds were dumb
While life was good for us but bad for some
We still hanker badly for what we lost.
A word, a thought, a slip of the tongue
Is more than enough in these current times
For the social police to cancel us.
Then poor souls who just craved verbal leeway
Seldom possess the natural right to live
Or converse and even to speak their mind.
For they are the pariahs of this world
Condemned to silence and never question
The prevailing wind, the drift, your truth.
Even the simplest features of before
Fail to answer to our clarion call
And so we suffer, hope, but always fall.

HARD ADVICE

All human courage is now required
To deal with life's hard realities

A life, a job, a mixture of woes
Coalesce into a mass of fear

The sheer blatant roughness of it all
Has an expectation of toughness

No room for snowflakes in this cruel world
No time for retrospective judgements

The need for robustness in our lives
Trumps the notions of perceived weakness

A life that is soon falling apart
Attracts no sympathy in these times

Be strong, be you, be all that we wish
Be just this and accept with relish

IN MEMORIAM

Whenever I think of Randy's life
One so gifted and enjoyable,
I wonder why we're even here
So pointless is his passing.
The thought of his giant beard
The sight of his serious smile
The odd American experience
All things I have witnessed
So complete remains my memory.
His careful and precise approach
Attests to scientific know-how
His talent was so clear to others
Yet so opaque to the man himself.
But our recall now persists in truth.

LAKE AND MOUNTAINS

My heart is warmed by the sight of beauty
The dark green forests radiate sweet light.
Almost as great are the majestic hills
Each one pregnant with secrets and sunshine.
All giants contain this solemn promise
That deep within resides some mystery
Which can slowly reveal its inner truth
So we can feel at ease with nature's will.

Down by the river's edge we look beyond
To distant islands too small for living
But good enough for the likes of grazers
Which now roam at will while we are sitting
In cosy glass-protected pleasure boats
And gaze beyond the limits of the lake
To hills that become mountains full of hope.
Such visions now inspire and then amaze.

LEGACY AND LIVING

Only living souls feel the benefit
Of great reputations and much respect
For all that is achieved during a life
That so embodies what is most admired.
Whether great music, art or written works
Whether the truth of science or new ideas
Whether anything achieved can change us
I rather doubt and others might agree.
But what difference does this truly make
To great figures now sadly laid to rest
Who never knew this retrospective awe
This strange obsession with all that is past?
To strive to leave a noble legacy
Benefits all mankind but not ourselves.

MAGIC MOUNTAIN

This rich tableau of fairy tale beauty
Points without effort to a cloudless sky
Broad vistas of tree-lined mountain sides
Coalesce in unison with grey mists
Each encircling bases of stone and earth
While broad swathes of elegant green forests
Adorn a noble vision of Arcadia
Now completing the sweetness of a dream

Ascending the gentle pathways and slopes
We feel some fragments of the sheer power
Of this strange and present natural place
This clear testament to evolution.
The mountain peak that seems so far away
Reminds us all of nature's mystery
The yellow sunlight shining down on us
Completes cycles of magic, you and me

MALIGNANT FUTURE

She now negotiates her life with care
While always knowing that her time is short
Keenly aware of space, time and the end
Of all that truly matters or transcends.
The malignancy that grows within her
Does not allow a choice of fear or dread
Though these twin horrors now beckon and threat.
Yet resist she must and resist she does,
Such courage arises within her soul
All that is left before a timely death
All that she hoped and dreamed of during life
All just a fantasy never to pass
Now that she sees so clearly what is lost
Now that the future has nothing to show.

MEDICAL EMERGENCE

The noble home of scholarship beckons
To all of us aspiring to lofty heights
To live and work among the brilliant
And the stricken in equal measure.
To cure or relieve the stressful
Pain and suffering of diverse souls
Is all but a memory of past ambition
The legacy of uncertain striving.

The Maltese cross of red brick excellence
Promises much in its hidden elegance,
Literally a Mecca to would-be doctors
Both those who will and others who fail
To match the rigorous standards set
By older practitioners of clinical mastery
The stylised history and examination
That so ably converts us into stereotypes.

But those who complain at any injustice
Who utter a jeremiad or clever rejoinder,
Those who question the wisdom of ages
Who are both the person and the doctor
Must always take especial note and care.
For to oppose traditions that time has forged
To raise the clever head above the parapet
Carries dangers that only fools may dare.

MEDICAL WISDOM

Only when I think of all the lives
I could never save despite my aim
To do what others could one day dream
Can I see the truth of this sad lie
That we as gods of life and living
The holy masters of survival
Have any power, now or later
To cure or reverse life's one cruel path

It took me three decades to convince
My colleagues, myself and those who cared
That we should be duly reconciled
With this dose of truth and more besides
A pain, a weakness plus dreadful fear
 Often comes our way to heal and calm
The wisdom of Hippocrates tells
Of kindness and drugs but do no harm.

MOON FEVER

He is only madness before the moon
Its unusual brightness reflects his pain
Now in its apogee

But the peak of sensation does not match
The closeness of the celestial sphere
A rare super moon.

Its red brown appearance is just a taste
Of the unsettling swings and future moods
The impending insanity

There comes a slow awareness of a dream
Of blood images, werewolves and much worse
To accompany his mood

Yet moonlight is spread all around the earth
Giving hope and succour to the stricken
As compassion works

But such help has arrived too late for man
The rational mind escapes forever
Leaving only despair

NIGHT WATCH

On waking from a mystic dream
I know the meaning of terror
The insidious creep of horrors
Deeply ingrained within my soul.
Yet I still wonder how it came
How it appeared at such a moment
How I coped with absolute fear
The kind that reduces you to ashes.
On waking in the morning sunlight
All fears and terrors now abated
I somehow fail to remember well
Just how awful I was made to feel
By some external force that gripped
My person and the very stuff of me.
Perhaps it was your only portrait
Smiling when it should have scowled
Angry when compassion was required
To calm my shattered insides out
To pour sweet balms upon my fate
That created the fear of loneliness
This disruptor of an inner calm

NOSTALGIC RIVER

Earth and deer roll before our eyes
As history unfolds in sporadic visions
This strange fusion of tree and life
Both pregnant with distant memories.
The winding river reflects the sunlight
And bathes our minds in tranquillity
The beauty of its quiet meandering
Does much to reinforce our calm
Our constant wish to travel back
And gain a former sense of normality.
But against these flights of magic
Of flashbacks to good old times
Soon we are transported to reality
As cars and caravans surround us.

OCEAN VIEW

Between the distant red horizon
And the subtle blueness of the sky
Lay the clear body of the ocean.
It's calm in places but rough elsewhere
The choppy water producing fear
For sailing boats and people swimming,
But they always swim against the tide.
Water graves provide such simple rides.

This tapestry of aquatic life
That so nourishes the ocean deep
Is now a sad testament to grief
To those poor children that someone loved
The spawn of a nation strong and proud
The clear growth of what was once so clear.
Yet this trauma seemed so worth the risk
And everything worthwhile seemed so near

Above the sea birds dive and observe
The unfolding stories down below
White dots of spume and froth rise between
The waves as they gather speed and height
All the while encircling those within
Its fatal embrace as they look doom
In the eye of the storm that slowly
Seals their fate and cruelly acts so soon.

Long boats have a better chance for sure
Than these flimsy relics of the past
The hope of a slow and steady course
Is duly shattered by tides and more.
Yet still they come and suffer the fate
Of souls with a promise of safety.
The now tattered remnants of a dream
Give no comfort to the many dead.

Distant visions of blue sea and sky
Might seem a first to promise beauty
To imbue us with a sense of pride
In its all movement and majesty.
But look further with a careful eye
While viewing life between wind and foam
When all the suffering splits the waves
In fragments of muscle, soul and bone

OUT OF THE WORLD

If all of us must forever die alone
Then all of life itself is lived alone.
However close and warmly loved we are
Or think that we are special in this life
Nothing else could be a greater falsehood
For in truth we are all defined by death
And if that goes badly then all is lost.

If a life is said to be one well lived
Then a badly lived death negates us all
For in this reality life and death
Are just two aspects of the one stark truth
That they just cannot be separated.
 Fear of life is equal to fear of death
And both of these have the power to kill.

Is there such a thing as life before death?
Can these two forces of the world around
And about our short sojourn on this earth
Ever revolve or evolve into joy?
The answer to that question eludes all.
The sad truth that is never truly known
Is that we live our lives and die alone

PONDERING CREATION

This subtle joke of great creation
Has spawned manifold explanations
Each one finely tailored to suit us
Each one surely destined to confuse.

How are we meant to choose the theory
That fits us best for our creed and brain?
Once early thoughts and lies abounded
And duly scared us stiff, one and all.

The truth eludes and proof deceives us
 Makes us blind to logic and the rest
But somehow the fragile intellect
Wins out despite the religious test.

Now we are sure and then we are not
This constant wavering of senses
Is just a symptom of our weakness,
Our tendency always to lose the plot.

RETROSPECTIVE JUDGEMENT

I am reduced to only half a person
Which always means two personas
One before this retrospective thought
And another in the here and now.
Which points to just one truth:
I've always bathed in mediocrity
I've only chosen the safest path
To rise above the common ground
To shine and sparkle above the rest
Of mice and men who dare to meet
My standards bearing just success.
Judgements made in thoughtful mode
Cause only pain and sad distress
Make a joke of inner speculation
This awful habit of retrospective guilt
And disappointment at achievements
All of which were justly won.
Am I making too harsh a judgement
Of this constant failure to rise
And grant my youthful aspirations?

ROUGH TRAINING

You sleep now without fear or conscience
Without memory or remorse for cruelties
And humiliations meted out as training
For trials that were yet to come ahead.
We meet now on such friendly terms
As if oblivious and changing the past
So it matches what we now experience
As if the previous trauma never existed
As if I never almost ceased to function
In this world or indeed the next.
I have a keen recall of past events
Of words and actions meant to help
But only served to make me suffer.
Such kindnesses remain and wound.

RUSTIC FERVOUR

A russet dusting of air and cornfields
Plays homage to neat arrays of grasslands
In this rustic place of country beauty
That does due justice to Hardy's vision.
Across the calm network of hay and bales
A flock of starlings sweep the light blue sky
Now adding truth to this authentic view
While never detracting from memory.

The gentle symmetry of brown green fields
Bordered on four sides by wooden limits
Raises the spirits of much depressed hearts
Restoring them to a life of wisdom.
A complex pattern lies before us
Combining alluvial plains and clay
Always hiding the lees of history
Such is the power of sight and silage.

Now a cornucopia of pleasures
Awaits the tourist and the resident
Both are subtly struck by the sights and sounds
Of this myriad of criss-crossed pastures.
Yet few outsiders know of the feedstock
So vital to machinery of farms
The harvester and the harvest seldom
Match the ignorant minds of visitors.

But some reversion to authentic times
Still has the power to restore old minds
Notions of cider among the locals
Conjures images of golden farm folk
A cup, some ale, a hearty meal and more
Now blending in some strange way with this truth:
However much we yearn for what has passed
We can never recapture times of yore

SEA BREAKER

All time now seems strangely suspended
In this relaxing reverie of sound
Echoes of childhood

Each rolling wave has colours of blue
Tinged with the whiteness of riding spume
Sparks our imagination

Impending breakers of ocean smoothness
Race ahead but never manage to touch
Our fears abated

The vista stretches for endless miles
Of sea, sand and golden promenades
Our wishes satisfied

Distant ships soon become magnified
Despite the enclosures held within
Good not to be there

Now what matters is the tranquil mood
That somehow manages to calm us
All is now quiet

SOULFUL VIRTUOSITY

We have the human capacity to feel
The virtuoso delights of gifted souls
Their wondrous gifts of huge dexterity
Enrapture first and then enrich us all.
The speed of movement across the board
Hardly seems to know its limits
So touchingly does the music beguile
Our range of sense and gentle mood.

Such talent emerging from the young
Is rich testimony to the art of life
The strange but clear inheritance
Of silent genes that find expression
In this flowering of keyboard skill
This sense of mystic spirituality
So suddenly emerging in the sounds
That makes us live the life we do.

The divine music that fill our hearts
And minds so moved by aural beauty
Arise from creators and performers
Both the conception and its actuation.
But listen carefully to the perfect pitch
The gentle cadence of human speech
The merging of words and sounds
Filling us with awe that must not speak.

SPORTS

We can practise all we want
Achieving what seems to others
An apparent pinnacle of work
A record of our noble art.
And so exists the self-deceipt
The almost certain knowledge
Of our realistic mediocrity
The bottom level of classier acts
That only serves to perpetuate
The proof of poor existence

Practice does not make perfect
Despite the wisdom of the times
Only listen to the truly great
And never worry about their trials
Just luxuriate in their genius
The fragrant music that emanates
From every corner of the world
And fills all souls with feeling.
These sports are of another kind
They truly belong to another time.

SUNSHINE RULES

Why are we so obsessed with sunshine?
Not the eternal light of our lives
The precious issues of our loving
But the shining sun above our heads
The visible source of warmth and grass.

We travel those miles to seek its glare
To feel first –hand its seductive side
But we're also warned to be aware
Of its power to destroy our sight
To maim, disfigure and maybe kill.

But still we seek what we never have
Nor ever will if we stay the course.
So we dream on in sad ignorance
Of all that warm weather can promise
Its gentle light rays lined with menace

But sunshine warmth and radiant light
Contain more than we can ever know
Even as we try to understand
It's strange but always friendly allure
It hides from us its true mystery.

THE MAGPIE

I saw the magpie pecking at the lawn
Oblivious to the lurking dangers
Arising from behind

Just a few yards away the noise of cars
Merges in ignorance with the bird song
Now barely audible

But on and on our little friend now feeds
On small tips of grass and what must be earth
Intermittent but driven

Soon a squirrel ventures close and friendly
Acknowledging the bird's sincerity
Apparent mutual respect

The magpie kindly offers a flower
To its friend, its partner in this strange game
But the gift is refused

Both bird and mammal cease this odd charade
This tragic parody of wild living
And scamper away.

THE OBSERVERS

A vast array of interstellar beauty
Awaits the vision of the chosen few
The theorist and the observers
All eyes fixed on nature's mysteries.
The collective power of many brains
The all-embracing sweep of machines.
Like telescopes that search the heavens
The physical extension of the eye
That first discoverer of the myriads
Of Stars that twinkle and entice
That promise so much information
Yet are somehow always out of reach.
All knowledge then becomes vicarious
We interpret but never really know.

THE PATIENT AND HIS FEAR

This man has no future of any kind
Except in our collective memories.
And no amount of carers in the world
Can ever ease the mental suffering
The bitter regret for what was not tried
The sad waste of a life without a peak.
As the claws and tendrils of cancer spreads
To those distant parts that we never know
The true horror of his malady shows.
The constant fear that does not speak its name
Only serves to magnify his pain and more.
Some will feel the treatment with its power
Is almost worse than the disease itself,
But it promises the desired effects
In gaining just a bit more existence
As living is sweet whatever its time,
A life, an outlier, a hopeful sign
Is all we can hope for when death is near.
Life and diseases can be short and sharp
But recall and pain never fail to fear.

THE PHYSICIAN

All worries must finally end here
This pure paragon of excellence
So we like to think.

The expectant patient before us
Thinks we are equivalent to Gods
But we are not.

Never should anyone be so fooled
As to consider us curers of ills
We only mitigate.

It is true that surgeons can remove
A lump, a mass, a cancer or worse
But that is rare.

We listen, we think , then try to act
In order to soothe the pain we see
But alas, not always.

Yes, we strive to do our best for sure
While always showing our compassion
But we seldom cure.

THE PLAYERS

First the fiddle and then the playing
The tune that always reaches our hearts
Our minds have no defence to speak of
So deep is the power of music.
The rousing cadence of a nation
That always serves its population.
But a wider public is inspired
By this strange cacophony of sounds
This timely meeting of old and new.
A sound, a note, and a chance to shine
Entrances us all despite the time
It takes but a moment to impress.
The whole world may be a kind of stage
But these players are among the best.

THE SEAFRONT

Once a paragon of beach and water
The old vista of golden sands is gone.
The seafront running across the ocean
Is all but obscured by endless joy rides
The memories of bygone years are done.

An atmospheric harbour of beauty
Still impresses with all its history
Even though a deadly plague once came here
Through a narrow porthole eaten by death
The pathway to extinction comes but twice.

Yet once a king loved to visit this place
Acting as a balm to soothe his madness
While making the air a cure for illness.
We keep our patriotic awareness
Always close to our hearts and mindful eyes.

So what remains of this sad history
Of illness, beauty and soulful longing
That delights and depresses troubled folk?
The sea, the sand and the mist just beyond
Coalesce in this one true mystery.

THE THROW

The final chapter of life can end well
Or badly you know how it all depends
On bad luck

If a dice is thrown then the odds are clear
It's Evens Stevens whatever you think
Of good luck

A life, a career marked by distinction
May have an unfair ignoble ending
Because life is cruel

But life is life and neither good nor bad
Just as death is only the end of life
That is reality

A hope, a prayer, then a leap of faith
Has the power to stop the fear of death
Some people are lucky

The dice may be random, the dread is great
But people seldom change in their beliefs
Their tendency to hate.

THEN AND NOW

Patterns of existence have all but changed
In this strange unknown underworld of ours
A glance, a hope and then a perception
That life and medicine could somehow meet
Could bridge the timeless gap of knowledge
And thereby heal the painful wounds of man.

How wrong we were but right at the timing
An era of doctors that ruled supreme
That somehow managed to mix and then match
Their patients' needs, their hopes and darkest fears
Strutting like peacocks some of them appeared
As they ruled their roosts and ignored their peers.

So what have we learned from these grey masters?
That medicine is an art without doubt
That admission of weakness at that time
Of drained emotions and external fear
Must never emerge or come to the fore
Though in our time this is no longer law.

THINKING

Thinking is such a dangerous pastime
For it has the capacity for fear.
Questioning every aspect of our lives
Can bring into focus our shortcomings
And so acquaint us with impending death.
There is a strange but well-tried antidote
To this terrible sense of not-being
This cruel alienation from the world
The odd suspension from reality,
And that is for us not to think at all

ABOUT THE AUTHOR

Peter G.E. Kennedy CBE, MD, PhD, DSc, is a distinguished clinician and scientist who held the Burton Chair of Neurology for twenty-nine years (1987-2016) at Glasgow University where he remains active in research and teaching as a Professor and Honorary Senior Research Fellow in the School of Psychology and Neuroscience. He also has two master's degrees in philosophy, has written ten previous novels, a book of poetry, a book of short stories, an award-winning popular science book on African sleeping sickness, and co-edited two textbooks on neurological infections. He has received numerous awards for his research work, most recently the Royal Medal of the Royal Society of Edinburgh (RSE). He is a fellow of both the Academy of Medical Sciences and the RSE.

Printed in Great Britain
by Amazon